Garden

Greetings

Unique Gifts To Layer In Jars

Jackie Gannaway

Published in Austin, TX by COOKBOOK CUPBOARD
P.O. Box 50053, Austin, TX 78763
(512) 477-7070 phone   (512) 891-0094 fax

ISBN 1-885597-30-4

Over 2 Million Copies Of Jackie Gannaway's Books Are In Print!

Artwork by Frank Bielac of Mosey 'N Me - Katy, TX

This book is part of the Layers of Love™ Collection from Cookbook Cupboard. All rights reserved.

ORDER OUR 40 BOOK TITLES FROM
COOKBOOKCUPBOARD.COM

Mail Order Information

To order a copy of this book send a check for $3.95 + $1.50 for shipping (TX residents add 8.25 % sales tax) to Cookbook Cupboard, P.O. Box 50053, Austin, TX 78763. Send a note asking for this title by name. If you would like a descriptive list of the nearly 40 fun titles in The Kitchen Crafts Collection, send a note, call, or fax asking for a brochure.

Phone 512 477-7070   Fax 512 891-0094

What is this book about?

This book has many gift ideas for people who like flowers, potpourri, candles, and crafts. Many are layered in canning jars for a festive presentation. The "jar" ideas have a jar drawn around them on the page (to locate them at a glance).

One of the most unique ideas in this book is Potpourri Candy Snack Mix on pg. 16. Make it in your kitchen from different cereals and candy melting discs. Delicious and unusual for a gift or to serve at a patio party or shower.

Also unique are the eight different, specialized potting soil blends layered in quart jars. These are given as gifts (alone or with a small plant and a 6" flowerpot). They are formulated for different kinds of plants - giving that plant the type of soil it needs. These recipes are on pages 8 to 15.

One soil blend (the "Top to Bottom!" Soil Blend on pg. 15) contains <u>everything needed to pot a plant</u>, including pebbles for drainage and decorative bark for the top - all in one jar!

For a complete listing of recipes included in this book, refer to the Index on pg. 32.

Information about Canning Jars

Canning jars are sold at grocery stores, hardware stores, discount stores (summer) and dollar stores. They come in cases of 12 and in many, many sizes. This book calls for wide mouth and regular quarts, wide mouth and regular pints and wide mouth and regular half pints. Be sure to get the type of jar the recipe calls for. In some of these recipes mayo jars can be used. It will tell you that at the recipe.

The simplest way to get jars is to go to the grocery store and ask them to order them for you. They can usually get any size you need in 3 days from their warehouse.

Just a Jar

Don't underestimate how special a gift becomes when it is put into a canning jar with a decorated lid. Fill a jar with Hershey's Kisses®, barrettes, jacks or marbles, fortune cookies, any simple little gift for an adult or child. Put on a label or gift tag using some of the ideas on pg. 4. Write little messages and fold them up and place inside the jar, too. Maybe even write a poem and attach it!

3

How To Decorate The Jars

1) Cover lid with a circle of fabric. Hold in place with a rubber band -tie on a ribbon or raffia bow. Hot glue a bit fiberfill under the fabric for a "puffy" look.

2) Tape flat lid onto the jar and place a circle of fabric over that. Screw on the ring to hold fabric in place.

3) Fabric is available to match any theme. For this book look for garden and floral fabrics, bird fabrics. See "Fabric Gift Tags" below to coordinate the fabric jar top with a fabric gift tag.

4) Cross stitch or appliqué the fabric for the lid.

5) Use wrapping paper or brown paper sack instead of fabric (rubber stamp the brown paper sack).

6) Coordinate fabric with the colors of mix in the jar.

7) Paint a design on the jar with paint for glass - or even a make it look like a stained glass or etched glass jar with the products available at crafts stores.

8) Paint individual decorations with stained glass paint onto waxed paper. Pull them off and press into place on the jar. They will stick until pulled off.

9) Use a seed packet for a "To-From" tag.

Fabric Gift Tags

Buy some garden or bird design fabric that has actual objects in the design that can be cut out. Buy some "Wonder-Under®" at the fabric store. Follow the instructions on the Wonder-Under to fuse the design onto a piece of heavy paper (white or color).

Use this as your gift card saying "To and From". Or use your computer to print out instructions onto colored cardstock and embellish that with a fused design from the fabric.

Optional: Use a fine line marking pen to make lines around the fabric appliqué that represent sewing "running stitches" or "blanket stitch" as an accent.

You are not covering the entire card with fabric - you are placing an object that you have cut out of the fabric at the top of the card, at the center of the card -wherever it is appropriate for your card.

You can cover one entire side of the gift card with fabric, fold it in half and use the non fabric inside to write your "To-From" message.

Match the fabric for gift card with fabric for jar top.

Gift Baskets

The ideas in this books are perfect for gift baskets. The jars of special soil blends can be given in a basket lined with moss and including a flowerpot and a plant. The gift tag can be written on a packet of seeds. Other ideas for baskets follow on this page.

Flowerpot Gift Container

Make a gift container by using a large flowerpot and saucer. Line the pot with moss, put in the gifts, turn the saucer upside down on top of the pot (making a lid). Tie saucer and pot together with raffia.

Rye Grass Easter Basket

Line a basket with heavy plastic. Place a 1" layer of pea gravel into basket. Top gravel with 3" of potting soil. Sprinkle heavily with rye grass seed (garden center or home center). Water lightly daily, keeping top 1/2" of soil moist.

This will sprout in a few days and will be 1" to 1 1/2" tall in 10 to 14 days. The basket will actually have 1" to 2" tall grass growing in it! Use it for a living Easter basket or for a centerpiece.

Mossy Flower Basket

Wire silk flowers in many places over the outside of an inexpensive basket. Fill in the rest of the outside of the basket with moss (crafts store or garden center) (hot glue on the moss). Cover the handle with flowers and moss. Tie on a coordinating bow. Line basket with moss. Use as a centerpiece with more silk flowers or fill with gifts.

Mossy Flower Pot

You will need real growing moss from nature or moss spores (garden center). Soak a clay pot in water. Paint it all over with yogurt or sour milk (use a paintbrush). Rub with the real growing moss you have found outdoors or with the spores you have bought. Keep pot in a dark place. Water every few days with water mixed with plant food - brush this on with a paintbrush. In about 1 month the mold will be growing on the pot.

Silk Flower Basket

Hot glue silk flowers all over an inexpensive Easter basket (include the handle). Tie on matching ribbons.

Garden Products Used in this Book

All of the ingredients for the soil blends can be bought at Wal-Mart, Home Depot and Garden Centers. Schultz® and Scotts® are two brands that are widely distributed. There are many other brands. These products are sold in small bags.

Bone Meal is a source of phosphate and is sold in small boxes or small bags.

Horticultural Charcoal is tiny pieces of charcoal. It is used for aeration and for drainage, in soil blends for orchids and in terrariums to keep air fresh.

Horticultural Hydrated Lime helps neutralize acid soils. It is soil in small bags.

Perlite is tiny foam beads that add lightness and aeration.

Potting Soil is sold in bags and is usually a blend of soil and soil amendments. Any bagged potting soil can be used in these recipes.

Potting Bark is very, very small bark chips for decorative purposes.

Ready to Use Peat Moss - The bag <u>MUST</u> say "ready to use" on it. Most peat moss has to be soaked in water and squeezed out before using. That will not work in these potting soil mixes. The "ready to use" peat moss has eliminated that step before it is put it in the bag.

Vermiculite is made from mica, a mineral, and is a lightweight addition to soil.

Amaryllis Bulb Gift

Buy an amaryllis bulb in the fall. Plant it in a 6" flowerpot with its "nose and shoulders" above soil level. (Use purchased potting soil or Potting Soil for Flowering Plants - pg. 11.) Water thoroughly once. Put a terra cotta saucer upside down on top of the pot making a lid.

Spray paint the pot and lid a bright color or paint designs on it if you like. Tie the lid and pot together with raffia. Give with instructions to "put in a light (not direct sun) place. Begin watering when it starts to sprout." It will bloom with several large amaryllis flowers.

For The Home

Garden Tablecloth

Place a white tablecloth (can be plastic) on the table . Sprinkle flower petals and leaves (silk or real) all over.
   Cover with another cloth of very sheer white fabric that you can see through.

Garden Window Treatment

Select a sheer white fabric. Sew on small to medium silk flowers, leaves and petals about 18" to 24" apart (just enough for an accent). Use as a valance loosely draped over a curtain rod.

Sweet Potato Plant in a Jar

Poke 3 toothpicks around the middle of a sweet potato. Place it in a wide mouth quart jar filled with water. The toothpicks will hold half the potato out of the jar. The other half rests in the water. In a week the sweet potato will sprout an ivy like vine that will grow for months. Change water every few days.

Simmer Scents

Apple Vanilla Simmer Scent

1 Tb. whole cloves	12 1" pieces of cinnamon stick
1 Tb. vanilla	8 drops apple scented oil

Orange Simmer Scent

1/4 cup dried or fresh orange peel, cut into small pieces	6 1" pieces of cinnamon stick
	1 Tb. whole cloves
	8 drops orange scented oil

Winter Pine Simmer Scent

1/4 cup dried pine needles	8 tiny pine cones
1/4 cup dried chopped cedar needles	1 Tb. whole cloves
	8 drops pine scented oil

Cinnamon sticks cost less at the crafts store than the grocery store. Get scented oils at the crafts store.

1. Mix ingredients well. Place in a baby food jar or other small jar. Or increase ingredients to fit in a regular half pint jar.
2. Sprinkle oil' into the jar.
3. Place lid on jar and decorate jar (pg. 4). Give a card that says: "Use 1 to 2 Tb. with water in a simmer pot or in a small pan of simmering water on the stove for a lovely scent. Can be reused several times."

Potting Soil Blend for Herb Plants

| 1/2 cup small gravel | 2 1/4 cups ready to use peat moss |
| 1 cup potting soil | 1 1/2 cups potting soil |

Optional: Add 2 tsp. horticultural lime on top of first soil layer, sprinkling around edge of jar so it is visible as a layer.

1. Place gravel into a wide mouth quart canning jar.
2. Continue layering each ingredient on top of soil.
   Press each layer firmly in place with your fingers.
3. Place remaining 1 1/2 cups soil into jar last, adding more or less to completely fill the jar..
4. Place lid on jar and decorate jar (see pg. 4).
5. Give with instructions below. Give an herb plant and a flowerpot along with jar of potting soil in a gift basket, if desired (see pg. 5).

Potting Soil Blend for Herb Plants

1. Empty soil from jar into large bucket or large flowerpot, leaving gravel in jar. Blend soil well with your hands or a garden claw.
2. Place gravel into a 6" flowerpot. Fill pot 1/3 full of soil.
3. Place an herb plant into pot and place remaining soil around plant.

This jar fills one 6" flowerpot.

Potting Soil Blend for Orchids*

1 1/2 cups potting bark,
(small bark chips)
1/4 cup perlite
1/2 cup horticultural
charcoal

1/4 cup perlite
1/2 cup ready to use peat moss
1 1/2 cups potting bark

1. Place 1 1/2 cups potting bark into a wide mouth quart canning jar.
2. Continue layering each ingredient on top of bark. Press each layer firmly in place with your fingers.
3. Place remaining 1 1/2 cups bark into jar last, adding more or less to completely fill the jar.
4. Place lid on jar and decorate jar (see pg. 4).
5. Give with instructions below. Give an orchid and a pot along with potting soil in a gift basket, if desired (see pg. 5).

*Not all orchids are planted the traditional way in a pot. Be sure you are giving the right orchid for this potting method.

Potting Soil Blend for Orchids

1. Empty jar into large bucket or large flowerpot. Blend well with your hands or a garden claw.
2. Use a 6" flowerpot. Put a rock or broken piece of a flowerpot over hole, fill pot 1/3 full of soil.
3. Place an orchid into pot and place remaining soil around plant.

This jar fills one 6" flowerpot.

Potting Soil Blend for Leafy Green Houseplants

1 cup potting soil
1/2 cup perlite
1 cup ready to use peat moss

1/2 cup perlite
1 1/2 cups potting soil

Optional: Add 2 tsp. bone meal to soil.

1. Place 1 cup potting soil into a wide mouth quart canning jar. Press down firmly.
2. Continue layering each ingredient on top of soil.
3. Place remaining 1 1/2 cups soil into jar last, adding more or less to completely fill the jar.
4. Place lid on jar and decorate jar (see pg. 4).
5. Give with instructions below. Give a plant and pot along with jar of potting soil in a gift basket, if desired (see pg. 5).

Potting Soil Blend
for Leafy Green Houseplants

1. Empty jar into large bucket or large flowerpot. Blend well with your hands or a garden claw.
2. Use a 6" flowerpot. (Place a broken piece of pot to cover the hole in pot.).
3. Place a leafy green houseplant into pot and place remaining soil around plant.

This jar fills one 6" flowerpot.

Potting Soil Blend for Flowering Plants

1 3/4 cups potting soil   1/3 cup perlite
1/2 cup vermiculite   1 3/4 cup potting soil
1/2 cup ready to use peat moss

Optional: Add 1 tsp. horticultural lime and 1 Tb. bone meal to soil.

1. Place 1 3/4 cup potting soil into a wide mouth quart canning jar. Press down firmly.
2. Continue layering each ingredient on top of soil.
3. Place remaining 1 3/4 cup soil into jar last, adding more or less to completely fill the jar.
4. Place lid on jar and decorate jar (see pg. 4).
5. Give with instructions below. Give a plant and a pot along with jar of potting soil in a gift basket, if desired (see pg. 5).

Potting Soil Blend for Flowering Plants

1. Empty jar into large bucket or large flowerpot. Blend well with your hands or a garden claw.
2. Use a 6" flowerpot. Put a rock or broken piece of flowerpot over hole, fill pot 1/3 full of soil.
3. Place a flowering plant into pot and place remaining soil around plant.

This jar fills one 6" flowerpot.

Potting Soil Blend for Cactus Plants

1 cup potting soil
1 cup sand
2/3 cup ready to use peat moss

2/3 cup sand
1 1/2 cups potting soil

1. Place 1 cup potting soil into a wide mouth quart canning jar. Press down firmly.
2. Continue layering each ingredient on top of soil.
3. Place remaining 1 1/2 cups soil into jar last, adding more or less to completely fill the jar.
4. Place lid on jar and decorate jar (see pg. 4).
5. Give with instructions below. Give a cactus plant and a pot along with jar of potting soil in a gift basket, if desired (see pg. 5).

Note: Another good cactus blend is: 2 1/4 cups sand, 1 1/2 cups potting soil and 1 cup vermiculite. Layer half of each ingredien at a time in a wide mouth quart canning jar making 6 layers.

Potting Soil Blend for Cactus Plants

1. Empty jar into large bucket or large flowerpot. Blend well with your hands or a garden claw.
2. Use a 6" flowerpot. Put a rock or broken piece of a flowerpot over hole, fill pot 1/3 full of soil.
3. Place a cactus plant into pot and place remaining soil around plant.

This jar fills one 6" flowerpot.

Potting Soil Blend for Pepper Plants*

1 1/2 cups potting soil   1/2 cup perlite
1/2 cup sand   1 1/2 cups potting soil
1/2 cup vermiculite

1. Place 1 1/2 cups potting soil into a wide mouth quart canning jar. Press down firmly.
2. Continue layering each ingredient on top of soil.
3. Place remaining 1 1/2 cups soil into jar last, adding more or less to completely fill the jar.
4. Place lid on jar and decorate jar (see pg. 4).
5. Give with instructions below. Give a pepper plant and a flowerpot along with jar of potting soil in a gift basket, if desired (see pg. 5).

*This soil is for any of the many varieties of small hot peppers that are grown and used for cooking.

Potting Soil Blend for Pepper Plants

1. Empty soil from jar into large bucket or large flowerpot. Blend soil well with your hands or a garden claw.
2. Fill a 6" flowerpot 1/3 full of soil. (Place a broken piece of pot to cover the hole in pot.)
3. Place a pepper plant into pot and place remaining soil around plant.

This jar fills one 6" flowerpot.

Soil Conditioner Blend

1 1/4 cups ready to use
  peat moss
1 cup vermiculite
1 cup perlite

2 Tb. bone meal (opt.)
1 tsp. horticultural lime (opt.)
1 1/4 cups ready to use peat
  moss

1. Mix the optional bone meal and lime into peat moss.
2. Place 1 1/4 cups peat moss into a wide mouth quart canning jar. Press down firmly.
3. Continue layering each ingredient on top of peat moss. Place remaining 1 1/4 cups peat moss into jar last, adding more or less to completely fill jar.
4. Place lid on jar and decorate jar (see pg. 4).
5. Give with instructions below.

Soil Conditioner Blend

1. Empty jar into large bucket or large flowerpot. Blend well with your hands or a garden claw.
2. Place soil conditioner back into jar to store.
3. Add 1 cup of this conditioner blend to 4 cups of commercial potting soil when potting house or patio plants.

"Top to Bottom!" Soil Blend

This has gravel for drainage, soil, and a decorative bark chip covering for the finished plant.

1/2 cup small gravel
1/2 cup perlite
1 3/4 cup potting soil
1/3 cup vermiculite

1/3 cup ready to use peat moss
1 1/2 cups potting soil
3/4 cup potting bark (small chips to decorate top of pot)

Optional: Add 1 tsp. horticultural lime and 1 Tb. bone meal to soil.

1. Place gravel into a wide mouth quart size canning jar.
2. Continue layering the next ingredients on top of gravel, pressing and smoothing each layer firmly in place.
3. Place potting bark chips in jar last, using enough to completely fill the jar.
4. Place lid on jar and decorate jar (see pg. 4).
5. Give with instructions below. Give a plant and a flowerpot along with this soil in a gift basket, if desired (see pg. 5).

"Top to Bottom!" Soil Blend

1. Remove bark chips from top of jar and set aside.
2. Empty soil from jar into large bucket or large flowerpot, leaving gravel and perlite in jar. Blend well with your hands or a garden claw.
3. Place gravel and perlite into a 6" flowerpot.
4. Fill flowerpot 1/3 full with soil mix.
5. Place a plant into pot and fill with remaining soil.
6. Top the soil with the decorative bark chips.

This jar fills one 6" flowerpot.

Potpourri Candy Snack Mix
This looks like potpourri and it is for eating!

4 cups Kix® cereal
4 cups Honeycomb® cereal
4 cups corn flakes cereal
food coloring

3 (14 oz.) bags of candy melting discs (Wilton® is one brand), white, medium green, and yellow*

* Divide package of white discs in half. Melt and color half lavender and the other half pink with food coloring. You will now have lavender, pink, yellow and green. (You can buy all white discs and color them as desired.) Melt each color as needed, toss with cereal - then melt the next color.

For planning large quantities - use 1/2 pkg. of candy discs for 3 to 4 cups cereal.

1. Melt green candy discs according to package directions (microwave is easy and fast).
2. Place 4 cups corn flakes in very large bowl or pot. Pour green melted candy coating over corn flakes and toss very, very gently so as not to break the cereal too much. Toss until all the corn flakes are coated with green. Spread this out on foil or waxed paper until dry.
3. Repeat this process, coloring the Kix cereal and the Honeycomb cereal 2 colors each.
4. Once the coated cereals are dry, break into as individual pieces as you can (nickel or quarter size or smaller). Blend all the coated cereals in your largest pot. Keep sealed in large gallon zipper bags or other airtight container until serving. This keeps 1 or 2 weeks.
5. To serve, place in a large clear glass bowl as a finger food. This is fun at a springtime baby or wedding shower.
6. To give as gifts, place in individual zipper sandwich bags or quart zipper bags. Tie on a card telling what it is and multi-colored ribbons to match the colors.

    You can also layer this in different colored layers in pint or quart jars (can be mayo jars) topped with matching fabric and ribbons.

    Select colors to match your theme. You should always use a green corn flake "leaf" - but you can include orange and bright yellow with it for fall - several shades of pink and red for Valentine's Day.

This recipe serves approximately 20 to 30 people or makes about 10 to 12 cups for putting in baggies or jars.

Gel Potpourri in a Half Pint Jar

1 cup liquid potpourri concentrate (simmering potpourri)

2 envelopes Knox® unflavored gelatin

1. Place liquid potpourri in a small pan. Heat to a simmer.
2. Turn off heat. Sprinkle gelatin into pan. Blend thoroughly with a whisk.
3. Pour into a regular half pint canning jar. Refrigerate for a quick set or leave out to set in several hours. Once set it will stay set without refrigeration.
4. Store with lid on. To use or give as a gift, remove flat part of lid and place a paper or lace doily over top of jar. Secure with either a rubber band and ribbon or by screwing the ring part of the lid.

Note: Use gel alone or layer seashells, pretty pebbles, marbles, etc. in jar before pouring in gel.

> This CANNOT be used as a gel candle.

Gel Potpourri in A Tea Cup!

Use an apple/cinnamon fragrance of simmering potpourri. Place the gel into a decorative floral pattern antique tea cup.

Use an epoxy glue to glue cup to a matching saucer.

Glue small silk flowers onto the handle and tie small silk ribbons onto the handle.

A room freshener that looks just like a cup of tea!

Garden Spoon

Glue flowers and ribbons into bowl part of a spoon and on handle. Match flowers and ribbons to the teacup. Place this spoon on the saucer for an extra accent.

Layered Potpourri In a Quart Jar

3 colors of purchased
  dried flowers (off white
  is also a good color)
1 or more kinds of green
  leaves from purchased
  dried flowers

2 Tb. vermiculite
12 drops potpourri
  oil

Use up all your "tired" dried flowers for this.

1. Break up flowers and leaves into small pieces (size of a quarter or natural size of a bud or leaf). Keep each color separate.
2. Place vermiculite in a small dish and mix in potpourri oil. Blend very well.
3. Place vermiculite in the bottom of a quart canning jar (or a mayo jar). The vermiculite will help hold the scent for a long time.
4. Alternate colors of flowers in layers until jar is full. Sprinkle flowers with a little more potpourri oil.
5. Place lid on jar and leave for several days up to a week or two for scent to permeate flowers.
6. When ready to use (or give as a gift), remove lid and place a lace doily or antique handkerchief over opening. Hold in place with the metal ring if using a canning jar or with a rubber band if using a mayo jar. Tie on a matching ribbon.

Other Varieties

Do the same thing with a pint or quart jar full of seashells or very mini pinecones and bits of pine greenery and red berries instead of flowers.

Can display this potpourri in a clear glass bowl.

Potpourri Night Light
in a Quart Jar

1 quart size wide mouth canning jar
3 cups of purchased or homemade potpourri (use recipe on pg. 18)

1 small string of tiny white Christmas lights
6" lace or crocheted doily
potpourri oil

1. Place Christmas lights in jar and arrange where they fill the entire jar with excess cord coming out the top of jar.
2. Fill jar with potpourri, carefully pushing and arranging so jar is full of potpourri and lights are visible. Sprinkle some potpourri oil onto the potpourri.
3. Place doily on top of jar, holding in place with the a rubber band and a ribbon.
4. Plug in for a lovely nightlight or a patio light. The heat of the bulbs release the scent of the potpourri.

Keep opening covered with foil until time to give as a gift to keep the fragrance strong.

Beach Glass Potpourri and Candle
in a Terra Cotta Saucer

6" terra cotta saucer (for a flowerpot - but just the saucer)
1 1/4 cups beach glass, (small bits of tumbled glass in asstd. colors -) crafts store
1/2 cup coarse ice cream salt (opt.)
2" - 3" candle (next size bigger than a votive candle) (See step 1 below for more info)
1 Tb. cinnamon
10 drops potpourri oil

1. Hot glue the candle to the center of the saucer. The candle needs to be unscented or be a similar scent to the potpourri oil. Color of the candle needs to coordinate with the terra cotta and beach glass.
2. Mix cinnamon and oil very well in a small dish and sprinkle into saucer. (It doesn't matter if the oil is a scent that smells good with cinnamon - the cinnamon will not be a noticeable scent - it just holds the scent of the oil for a long time.)
3. Mix beach glass and coarse salt. (You don't have to use salt - you can use all beach glass - it depends on your budget - the salt is an inexpensive filler.) Place this mixture around candle, filling saucer. Sprinkle a little more potpourri oil onto the beach glass. Place this saucer into a gallon size zipper freezer bag and zip shut. Leave closed until time to use (several days to a week or more).
4. This is a lovely, unique, and fragrant gift to give to someone to use on a patio (or indoors).

Sea Shell Potpourri and Candle
in a Terra Cotta Saucer

Use the procedure above with seashells instead of beach glass.

Rose Hips, Dried Orange Slices
and Candle in a Terra Cotta Saucer

Use the procedure above with rose hips and dried orange slices instead of beach glass.

Sand Art Candle in a Pint Jar

1 pint size wide mouth   food coloring
    canning jar   votive candle
2 cups sand

1. Divide sand into 3 portions (use empty margarine tubs or similar).
2. Color 2 portions different colors with food coloring.
3. Place sand in jar alternating colors. Stop about 1 1/2" from the top of the jar.
4. Make a "sand art" design if desired by using a plain table knife or popsicle stick to push down into the sand along sides of the jar, allowing some of the colored sand to fall into spiked patterns.
5. Push votive candle into sand, leaving top of candle even with top of jar.
6. Finish filling around the candle with sand.
7. Keep lid on jar until ready to use.

Terrarium in a Quart Jar

1. Place 1" of gravel in bottom of a wide mouth quart canning jar.
2. Add 2" potting soil on top of gravel.
3. Add 4 pieces of horticultural charcoal (to keep air fresh).
4. Use a stick to poke holes for 1 or 2 small green plants. Gently drop plant into place and cover roots well with soil.
5. Add a few pebbles, marbles or a small ceramic figure for interest.
6. Sprinkle lightly with water. Place lid on jar.
7. Keep in a bright light (not direct sun).
8. If it gets too wet, remove lid for a day or two.
9. If it gets too dry, add a few drops water.
    (Can use a gallon jar instead.)

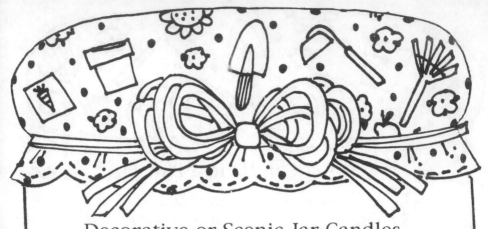

Decorative or Scenic Jar Candles

clear glass votive holder, shaped like a flowerpot*

regular quart or pint canning jar or a mayo jar (not wide mouth)

decorative items to put in the jar

votive candle

*These are readily available at crafts stores, import stores and discount stores.

This is what you will be making:

Place the votive holder in opening in top of jar. It will sit there, forming a "stopper" for the jar. Put a votive candle in this holder. When the inside of the jar is decorated you will then tie a 1 1/2" wide ribbon around the neck of the jar.

The ribbon, candle, and jar contents need to coordinate in color. You can hot glue the votive holder in place to make permanent or leave it loose to change the jar contents later.

You will have a very pretty jar filled with whatever you can imagine topped with a colorful ribbon and a votive candle.

This item can be used at your house, given as a gift, sold at a bazaar, given as a party favor.

These can be done for any holiday, any theme, any color.

Page 23 has some examples of what you can put in the jar.

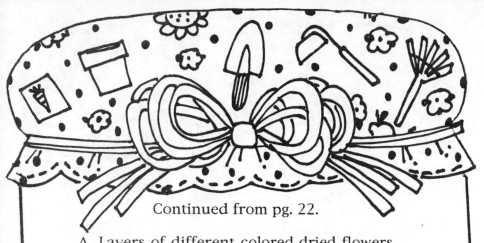

Continued from pg. 22.

A. Layers of different colored dried flowers.

B. Layers of pine cones, red berries, pine greenery.

C. Layers of candy corn, red hots, jelly beans. (Do for Halloween, Easter or Valentine's Day with layers of appropriate candy, seasonal ribbon and a matching votive.)

D. Layers of dried orange peel and cinnamon sticks.

E. Layer different small types of seashells. Even place the very tiny seashells in the votive holder around the votive candle.

F. Make a "scene" in the jar: (Hot glue components into place.)

Scenes can be:

Fake decorative snow, a little plastic snowman and a plastic pine tree.

An Easter scene with Easter grass, a bunny and eggs.

A Christmas tree, gifts and Santa.

Personalize a jar scene to your school, church, club, Brownies, Cub Scouts, or office using appropriate materials and the right color of ribbon and votive.

Ice Jar Candles

pint wide mouth
canning jar
distilled water
votive candle

fresh or dried flowers
and leaves
very small paper cups
like bathroom cups)

1. Tape a small paper cup evenly in the center of the mouth of the jar. Tape it on each of four sides. Place a few pebbles or other weights into cup. This will become the hole in the ice into which you place the votive candle.
2. Fill jar with small flowers and leaves (silk or real).
3. Fill jar with water, not putting any in the paper cup. Place lid on jar.
4. Freeze jar several hours or overnight.
5. Remove paper cup and insert a votive candle in the space. Put lid back on jar and keep this all in the freezer until ready to use. This stays frozen several hours at room temperature so you have plenty of time to deliver it as a gift.

This candle can be used inside the jar or can be maneuvered to come out of the jar and stand alone as a candle of ice.

Distilled water makes a clearer candle, but tap water is fine.
Put some warm water in jar to loosen paper cup.

Vary the flowers with the season. Pine greenery and red berries in the winter - spring flowers in the spring - daisies in the summer.

Ice Rings

Freeze a ring mold with edible flowers, cranberries, pieces of herbs, etc. Float in a punch bowl. Freeze in thirds. Fill 1/3 full of water - freeze that. Put in some of the flowers and add more water. Freeze again. Repeat with more flowers and top it off with ice and freeze.
Place in a bowl of warm water to unmold.

Ice Wreath

Use a ring mold as described above, adding winter greenery and berries. Hang this wreath outside in the winter (or in the summer!)

Ice Decanter

Cut off the bottom 2/3 of a 2 liter plastic soda bottle or use a half gallon paper milk carton.
Place an empty wine bottle of the same size you plan to serve into the soda bottle or milk carton. Weight bottle down by filling part way with dried beans. Place 2 inches of water into the bottom of container.
Place flowers, berries, herbs, winter greenery, spring flowers - whatever fits the occasion.
Freeze. Fill to top with water and refreeze.
Twist bottle under running warm water to unmold.
Keep decanter frozen until ready to use. Place a bottle of wine into decanter and serve wrapped with a white cloth napkin to absorb drips.

Ice Bowls

Use a metal mixing bowl. Place a big margarine tub or Cool-Whip®c container in the center. Tape container in place with 4 pieces of tape. Fill bowl 1/3 full of water. Place greenery and flowers in place. Freeze. Fill to top with water and refreeze.
Use a little warm water to remove container. Fill bowl with flowers or even fruit salad.

Mint Ice Cubes

Fill ice trays 1/3 full of water. Place mint leaves in ice cubes. Freeze. Finish filling with water and freeze. Serve in lemonade or iced tea.

Scented Bath Salts or Bath Crystals

1 cup Epsom salts (phar-
  macy) OR sea salt cry-
  stals (grocery store)
4 drops potpourri oil or
  perfume

food coloring
Opt: 1 tsp. glycerin
  or 2 Tb. mineral
  oil (pharmacy)

1. Place Epsom salts or sea salt crystals and optional glycerin or mineral oil in bowl. Add oil or perfume. Stir well to thoroughly blend fragrance.
2. Separate salt mixture into three parts, placing each part in a small dish.
3. Color two of the dishes of salt with food coloring (leave one dish white) - you will now have 3 colors.
4. Use a regular HALF pint canning jar (8 oz.) or any decorative clear jar or bottle as long as it has a fairly wide opening at the top. (Mayo jar will work.)
5. Place one of the colored layers into the jar, followed by the white layer and topped by most of the final color.
6. If desired, take a plain table knife and press into the salts from top to bottom in several places around the edges, making a "sand-art" design.
7. Top jar with remaining salts so salts are completely to the top.
8. Decorate lid of jar (see pg. 4). Give in a basket with Scented Bath Powder (pg. 27).

Recipe continued on pg. 27.

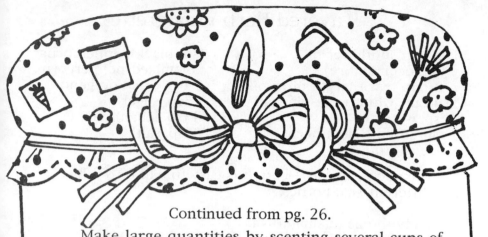

Continued from pg. 26.

Make large quantities by scenting several cups of Epsom salts and then coloring into 2 colors and white. Then measure 1/3 cup of each color into jars. Each jar takes 1 cup, so you can plan to fill 4 jars, 8 jars, etc. and scent and color all the salts you will need first.

Give with a card that says: "Mary's Special Bath Salts" or "Shalimar Bath Salts". Write: "Sprinkle 2 to 3 Tb. into your bath water."

Scented Bath Powder
In a Half Pint Jar

2/3 cup cornstarch   6-8 drops potpourri oil
1/3 cup baking soda   or perfume

1. Place cornstarch and baking soda into a bowl.
2. Add oil or perfume. Stir very well to completely blend in the fragrance.
3. Place in a half pint wide mouth jar (a short low jar).
4. You can include a powder puff. Buy a small flattish one at the make up counter of the discount store or grocery, Place it in a thin baggie or wrap in plastic wrap and place in jar on top of powder.
5. Place lid on jar. Decorate jar including a label that says "Rose Bath Powder" or "Shalimar Bath Powder". It is particularly pretty to hot glue on a silk rose or gardenia and tie a matching ribbon around lid of jar.

Make this at least two weeks ahead. Or scent a large quantity of powder and leave it sealed for 2 weeks before putting into individual jars.

Layered Herb Vinaigrette

1/3 cup sunflower oil,
(grocery store)
1/3 cup extra virgin olive oil
1/4 cup white wine vinegar
2 tsp. water
1 tsp. dried Italian herb
seasoning

1 tsp. black peppercorns
or mixed peppercorns
1/2 tsp. dried oregano
1/2 tsp. sugar
1/4 tsp. lemon pepper
1/8 tsp. salt

This recipe makes 1 cup. It is easy to half or double for different size bottles.

1. Mix both oils in small dish.
2. Mix all dry ingredients in another small dish.
3. Add dry ingredients to oil mixture. Blend well.
4. Use an 8 oz. (1 cup) small tapered bottle that is larger at the bottom than the top (import stores) or a narrow, tall straight bottle. The oil and vinegar stay separate (in 2 layers). This type of narrow bottle makes the most visible impact.
5. Using a funnel, pour vinegar and water into bottle.
6. Pour oil/herb mixture into jar on top of vinegar, using less oil or more oil if necessary to come to top of bottle.
7. Cap bottle and tie raffia around neck. You can also dip the top of the capped bottle into colored, melted candle wax for a pretty wax seal and then tie on raffia.

Give a card with instructions below:

Herb Vinaigrette

Shake well. Sprinkle over salads, sliced tomatoes, raw or cooked vegetables. Use to marinate chicken or fish.

Herb Vinegar Kit in a Half Pint Jar
(Give this kit-the recipient will make herb vinegar!)

1 half pint regular
   canning jar
1 cup white wine vinegar

1/2 cup mixed snipped
   fresh herbs (like oregano,
   marjoram, chives,
   tarragon, basil)

1. Fill jar with vinegar. Tape flat lid into place.
2. Snip fresh herbs into tiny pieces*. Place 1/2 cup herbs into a thin sandwich bag (not zipper type).
3. Place flat lid on canning jar. Place baggie of herbs on top of flat lid, spreading to cover top of jar. Screw ring part of lid onto jar to hold herb bag in place.
4. You now have a little plastic "pillow" full of herbs attached to the top of jar.
5. Tie on a ribbon or raffia and attach instructions below:

*Note: Everything can be done weeks or months ahead, including putting vinegar in jars, preparing instruction cards, cutting the ribbons to lengths - BUT NOT putting herbs on jars. Do that one day ahead so the herbs will be fresh.

Please make right away while the herbs are fresh!

Herb Vinegar
1. Place herbs in a small bowl. "Bruise" herbs by pressing them with a spoon.
2. Warm the vinegar (microwave or stove top) -don't let it simmer or boil - just warm it.
3. Place herbs back in jar. Add warm vinegar.
4. Steep for 2 weeks, shaking jar occasionally.
5. Strain vinegar through a coffee filter, discarding herbs. Place vinegar back in jar.
6. Use this herb vinegar to make salad dressings, sprinkle on beef or chicken before grilling, sprinkle onto raw or cooked vegetables. Add a Tb. to soup or stews.

"Dramatic" Silk Flower Arrangements

Layering in Vases

Fill a clear vase with marbles, rocks, mini pinecones, dried flowers, cranberries, birdseed - any thing that goes with your theme. Fill vase full or part way. Certain things like marbles can be used with water and fresh flowers. Other things like mini pinecones need to be used with no water and silk flowers. This also looks good with small branches in place of flowers.

Holiday Layering in Vases

Fill a clear vase as described above with appropriate holiday items (Halloween candies, mini Christmas balls, the "message" Valentine candies, Easter eggs). Place a bare tree branch of the correct shape and size in the vase and hang holiday decorations from it.

Acrylic "Water" in Vases

Crafts stores sell a two part mixture that is used to pour into a clear vase into which you have placed silk flowers.

The mixture hardens solid and clear and looks like real water.

Water Absorbing Crystals in Vases

Crafts stores sell tiny packages of crystals that look like rock salt. When soaked in water the crystals make a gallon of soft, squishy "blobs".

These can be colored with food coloring and used in clear vases for real flowers or silk flowers. Color with food coloring and make colored layers in the vase, leave clear, or use one solid color for the whole vase. These crystals are very interesting to see in arrangements and add a whole new dimension. When left clear they look like finely crushed ice.

Push an "item" into the middle of the crystals - it will look suspended.

Add liquid or simmering potpourri to the crystals for a scent. There are thorough instructions on the packages.

Feed The Backyard Birds In A Jar

songbird bird seed   wild bird seed
parrot blend bird seed

These three types of birdseed are varied in type of seed and look good layered in jars.

The songbird bird seed has many black sunflower seeds. The wild bird seed has mostly very small round millet seeds.

The parrot blend has very colorful seeds.

Layer 3 or 6 alternating layers of different seeds in a wide mouth quart jar (or a quart mayo jar). (You can also use a pint jar.) Use only a small amount of parrot food - it is more of an accent than a practical bird seed for the neighborhood birds.

Tape flat lid down and then screw on ring. Decorate jar with bird printed fabric, tie with raffia and maybe glue on a small feather bird.

Give with a card that says "Feed the Birds!" - Give with a birdfeeder, if desired.

Feed The Backyard Birds In A Birdfeeder

Instead of layering seeds in a jar layer them in a plastic tubular type of birdfeeder.

Assemble the bird perches as the directions say. Tape openings closed with Scotch tape. Pour the above 3 types of birdseed into feeder in layers. Tie raffia on the handle and give the feeder full of layered colors and varieties of seed.

Firefly Jar

Take a quart jar (can be a mayo jar). Poke holes for ventilation in the lid or put a piece of net over the opening. Decorate a label with rubber stamps, stickers, clip art, freehand. Write: "My Fireflies" or "Susie's Fireflies" or "Johnny's Fireflies". on the label. Give this to a child in summer at firefly season. He can keep some fireflies in the jar overnight to light up his room.

Bug Jar

Prepare jar as described for Firefly Jar above. Place a small branch and a few leaves into jar. Give to a child who will catch a caterpillar, a grasshopper or a spider for the jar. He will then observe it for a week and then release it (feeling it a fresh leaf and a couple of drops of water every day or two).

Index